Talking to Squirrels

Poems by Michael Hathaway

Kansas City   Spartan Press   Missouri

Spartan Press
Kansas City, MO
spartanpresskc@gmail.com

Copyright © Michael Hathaway, 2019
First Edition 1 3 5 7 9 10 8 6 4 2
ISBN: 978-1-946642-98-1
LCCN: 2019932512

Design, edits and layout: Jason Ryberg
Cover image: R.W. Leathem
Title page image: Jon Lee Grafton
Author photo: Alexis Rhone Fancher
All rights reserved. No part of this publication may be reproduced or transmitted in any form or by any means, electronic or mechanical, including photocopying, recording or by info retrieval system, without prior written permission from the author.

Some of these poems and stories first appeared in unrevised versions in *Beggars & Cheeseburgers; Chance Magazine; Chiron Review; Contrarywise: An Anthology (Kings Estate Press); 5 AM; Gargoyle; Home Planet News; Mad Rush; Mojave River Review* (on-line); *Nerve Cowboy; The Orange Room* (on-line); *The Plowman* (Canada); *Prairie Connection; Prairie Ink; Re) Verb; 22-5; Unexpected Harvest: A Gathering of Small Blessings* (Kings Estate Press); *Waterways: Poetry in the Mainstream*; and the limited edition chapbook *St. John Pastoral* (Casa de Cinco Hermanas Press, 2012).

CONTENTS

About Heaven / 1
Adam Had 'Em / 3
Attempt to Explain Loss / 4
The Ballad of Gypsy Rose / 5
The Big Picture / 9
Birthright / 10
What the Calendar Didn't Tell Me / 11
Cognitive Dissonance, or probably why
   people love coffee / 12
Cooking Secrets / 13
Deconstructing the Patriarchy / 16
Election 2012 / 17
Enlightenment / 18
Epitaph / 19
At the End of the Day / 20
About Equality / 21
Fleas / 22
Fore! / 23
Found Poem ... / 24
Full Circle / 25
How It Happens / 27
Leapfrog / 29
Letter to Mother, 7 Years Later,
   Postmarked Home / 32
Letting Go / 41
Love Light / 43
Medicare for All / 44
Memo to Craig ... / 45

Messenger / 46

Monster / 47

You Know You're Loved When People Are Willing
   to Give You the Moon / 48

My Best Friend Julie Pops Into a Dream In Progress
   a Year After Her Death / 50

The Non-smoker's Right / 51

One of Cassandra's, er, I Mean Mother's Dire Prophecies
   Actually Comes True / 52

The Perfect Tape / 54

Proposed Legislation: Never to Forget / 56

Question for the Federal Communications Commission / 57

Road Trip: Topeka, November 29, 1997 / 59

Rush Hour Traffic Jam / 61

St. John Pastoral / 62

What She Never Told Anyone / 63

Sometimes the Most You Can Do is Tend Your Own
   Little Corner of the World / 65

Symptomatic ... / 66

Talking to Squirrels / 67

They Don't Write Love Stories Like This Anymore / 69

Threshold / 70

Tracy Pops Into a Dream Two Years Later
   Just to Let Me Know / 71

Throwing Dirt: Remembering Julie / 73

A Toast / 82

Winter Snapshot 2011 / 84

For Ruth, my favorite poet.

About Heaven

If there are any heavens,
I'll get one –
not because my life was saintly,
or I did everything I *should* have done,
or didn't do what I *shouldn't* have done,
or believed a bunch of crap, or didn't –
but simply that every soul who suffers
this clumsy, tragic material mess
deserves a heaven.

I'd choose a simple heaven,
a small wood frame house way out in the country,
where it's always spring or autumn,
with rolling grass that is never mowed,
lots of trees in the distance
and a stream nearby.

The soul of every cat I ever knew will live there,
two rabbits named Melba and George,
two hens named Henny Penny and Penelope Beaker,
and five big rowdy dogs.

They'll all get along famously.
There will be no telephones, televisions or computers,
no automobiles or cowboys,

no religion, guns or money,
no sovereign boundaries,
no municipal laws or dreaded sickness,
no fleas or cat diseases.

There will be no people at all, except Mom
and a friend to visit now and then –
but they will be carefully screened –
and may not be
who they think they are.

Adam Had 'Em

The naming of the beasts is exhausting.
After 80+ cats in 20 years,
I am running out of names.

Christmas Eve, 2000,
I took in three unnamed female cats
disguised as *baby-sitting* for a friend.
When I realized it was permanent,
at first it seemed I might have to
resort to Fluffy and Snowball and Precious ...

But fate stepped in
the day I decided to administer
de-worming pills.

As I stood there exhausted,
bleeding and utterly defeated,
their names came down
like 40 whacks:

Lizzie
Lucrezia
& Lilith

Attempt to Explain Loss

A tall square plastic basket on my desk
serves as *Chiron Review*'s "In" box.

It was given me 25 years ago by my friend Pamela
as she packed for one of her myriad escapes from Kansas.

A few years ago, she called me out of the blue
after I hadn't heard from her in years.
We chatted four hours away.
She told me about her new apartment and puppy in Iowa.
I was in one of my many ill-fated attempts to escape Kansas,
this time I believe it was Joshua Tree. I told her about that.
We promised with much animated enthusiasm
to visit each other after we each got settled.

She died in her sleep two weeks later.
Pam is gone now, so are her sisters and our mothers,
anyone who would have cared in the slightest that
she's the one who gave me that basket.

The Ballad of Gypsy Rose

in memory of Connie Star (1948-2017)

On Sunday, July 2, around 9 a.m. my friend Connie Star took a swan dive into that Great Chocolate Fountain in the Sky. She's probably doing the backstroke even as we speak. I'm tempted to tell the story of her life, which is fascinating, and which she always wanted me to do. But that would be a bit overwhelming so soon after her passing, so instead, I'll tell the story of how we met and share a glimpse into the person she was.

In February, 1984, I was 22 years old, worked during the day as a typesetter at the daily newspaper and inhabited a trailer house on Maple Street in Great Bend, Kansas. (I'd also been publishing *The Kindred Spirit*, which would morph into *Chiron Review*, for two years.) I had a house full of roommates who wouldn't work or help with any expenses. They ran up the phone bill, let my cats out, magically appeared on my payday, then magically disappeared when the money was gone a few days later.

On February 4, at 3 a.m., one of my roommates woke me to say, *My friend Connie's on the phone, she wants to meet you. It's collect ...* I grumbled, stumbled to the phone and mumbled, *Hello?* The voice on the other end said, *Hi! I'm Gypsy Rose! Patty says you write poetry! I write poetry too! Listen!* She recited a poem she had written.

Then she said, *I sing too! Some people say I sound just like Janis Joplin, listen!* She sang every verse of, *I Gave My Love a Cherry (The Riddle Song).* It was one of those rare magical moments in life when time seems to stand still. I was utterly mesmerized by her voice. She had a deep, robust, intense alto voice that set off sparks, very much like Janis Joplin's did, the kind of bluesy, whiskey-laced voice you hear in smoke-filled barrooms. We talked and talked and talked until the alarm clock rang for me to get ready for work at 7 a.m. She promised to come visit, but I didn't expect to ever meet her.

Three days after that phone call, a knock came at my front door. There she stood, all 250 animated pounds of her. She had long, flowing, bright red hair adorned with colorful roach-clip feathers, light green cat eyes that saw directly into your soul, and a brown suede jacket with the fringe just swinging! She wore multiple necklaces, bracelets, long dangling earrings and a ring on every finger. She sparkled and jangled and said, *Hi! I'm Gypsy Rose!* She burst in, made herself at home, and dumped the entire contents of her oversized hippie fringe suede bag on my kitchen table. That's when the stories started. That's how the friendship of a lifetime was born.

She moved in with us, but my other friends were so jealous and so mean to her she moved right back out after three days. She didn't stay long enough to pay rent, but gave me her Beatles *White Album* in exchange for staying there and a few phone calls. I tried to refuse it, but she insisted.

A couple weeks later, I saw her in the grocery store. We chatted a bit. Even though she was homeless and had become an expert at surviving and living by her wits, she never told a lie or stole a single thing in her life. She knew I was having serious troubles with my *friends*. She pulled the food stamps from her wallet and counted them out. She gave me half of them, which I think was about $8 worth. Again, I tried to refuse, but she insisted. That's when I knew for sure she was a keeper.

She's the first person I came out to. It was a matter of self-defense, she was determined to marry me. I worried about losing her friendship, but coming out to her made our bond even stronger. She said I spoiled other men for her. She called me her *honorary husband*. We celebrated our anniversaries on most Valentine's days and sent each other *husband* and *wife* Valentine cards. She declared a few years ago we were the hillbilly version of *Will & Grace*. I liked that.

We were best buddies for 33 years. We both loved being where the people and the parties were, but neither one of us were ever interested in recreational drugs. We did a little drinking early on, but got bored with it. We didn't care what anyone else might indulge in as long as we could be at the party. And of course, it wasn't all smooth sailing. Neither one of us knew what a *boundary* was. We could argue and fight like cats. But even in the throes of our worst caterwauling, we both knew our friendship was forever, no matter what.

In her next incarnation, I'm thinking she'll be the benevolent and beloved queen of a small country. She had a serious *queen complex* and practiced for it all this lifetime. Wherever she lived was always a gathering place, where she held court and counseled anyone who needed counseling. She was awake and available late into the wee small hours of the night, and prevented more than one suicide in her life.

I really hate to see her go. I find myself still checking

my phone first thing in the morning for text messages from her. Sadness is inevitable, but so is gratitude. An epic friendship like this is one of life's greatest gifts. I'm ever so grateful to the Powers That Be that we met and were able to live out such an incredibly long and loyal friendship, to experience such powerful love.

The Big Picture

In the Stafford County Museum Library,
The History of Christianity
sets squarely between
Bulfinch's Mythology
and another book titled
Acts of War.

Birthright

My horoscope declares,
*Your father will be able to
leave you very little.*

When my father remarried and moved across town,
he gave me a little house on two acres,
the house I grew up in,
the safest place on earth,
where Mother's ashes are planted
and the remains of every pet
I ever loved.

Along with an armful of Hank Williams, Sr.
and Connie Smith records,
this came with a lifetime of lessons by example
in integrity, a work ethic beyond reproach,
and an undeniable sense that I was loved
no matter what.

What the Calendar Didn't Tell Me

The calendar told me that today the sun was in Scorpio,
that today was a regular work day,
that it was volunteer day and trash day at the museum;
that it was time to refill my prescription for Famotidine;
that I needed to make an appointment with the mechanic
to get my car repaired.

The calendar told me that four good friends
are celebrating birthdays this week
as well as Calvin Klein and Indira Gandhi;
that today I would teach an elderly widowed friend
how to pump gas at the self-service station after work;
that the cell phone and gas bills would arrive in the mail.

The calendar did not tell me that today
would be the last day I would ever see you alive.

Cognitive Dissonance, or
probably why people love coffee

Some nights misery piles on misery,
decades of loss and grief,
cruel and chronic depression,
tectonic plates of existential angst.

A country bumpkin in Sam Brownback's rural Kansas,
has no business
even knowing what that is.

And then there was that little quest for wisdom –
it really opened up a can of worms –
I eagerly & naively popped the top right off The Void,
peeked into the nihilists' abyss.

It's too late to un-see it now.
I'm that Looney Tunes character
free-falling endlessly,
seated at a bistro table, legs crossed,
calmly enjoying a nice cup of tea,
reading a good book
while everything never stops falling.

But all is well.
Time and age teach
All this silly horror
dissipates with the morning sun,
chores, and hot black coffee.

Cooking Secrets

In spring 1999, my best friend met "Richard From Burbank" through an on-line lonely-hearts ad. Richard From Burbank invited him to California so they could meet in person. My friend was hesitant to go alone, so this potential new amour paid my way to accompany him.

Richard From Burbank turned out to be decent, fun and interesting with decent, fun and interesting friends, with names like Carol, Andrea and Mother Don, a big burly baritone bartender at Venture Inn.

On Saturday night, Andrea, offered to make everyone dinner at Richard's house. She was a large and lovely fiftysomething transvestite, most exquisitely dressed and made-up. She invited my friend and I to accompany her to the market in her neighborhood. In the car, she said, *It's not safe. You stay behind me!* So there was this plus-size drag queen in a short, tight, bright hot pink skirt and high heels with two Kansas country boys following meekly in-tow.

The moment we entered the store, she transitioned. Her dainty walk turned into a macho, bow-legged swagger. She puffed out her chest and swung her arms. We followed her single file through the store as she compared prices and shopped for dinner. We survived our sojourn into the *bad neighborhood,* and returned to Richard's house.

While the others talked, laughed, and drank cocktails on the patio, I stood at the kitchen island and listened to Andrea talk as she prepared the food. She laid out great slabs of beef steak, peppered both sides until they were black, then attacked them ferociously with a stainless steel meat hammer. She said, *This is the secret to good steak,* and eyes twinkling, *This is how you beat your meat!*

She pounded those steaks over and over and over. As she pounded, she talked. She said, *So you're a writer? Maybe you will write my story?*

She hadn't seen her parents since she was 16. They disowned her and threw her out of their house when she came out of the closet. Andrea was homeless in San Francisco until Janis Joplin and her blond lady lover took her into their apartment. Andrea said Janis was very sweet to her.

Andrea had an affair with an actor who starred in a popular musical sitcom in the early 1970s. He was so sweet and sexy and she was so in love, she lost herself in him. But the sitcom's producer didn't want a transvestite hanging around his teen heartthrob star. Andrea explained she was a threat to '70s sitcom *family values* – meaning studio profits. The producer threatened one way or another, she would *disappear.* Fearing for her life, she did disappear.

Her eyes filled with tears. She said she wished she'd known then that nothing they could have done to her would have been worse than disappearing without saying goodbye, without telling her boyfriend why she left.

The more she talked, the more the tears ran, the angrier she got, the harder she pounded those poor steaks.

Maybe her stories were true, maybe not, I don't know. What I do know is those were the most tender steaks in the history of cooking – and the pain in her eyes was real.

Deconstructing the Patriarchy

For Linda Bloodworth-Thomason

Why do men strut around like cocks of the walk –
their egos ever-spewing geysers –
when women are the makers of life
& men are mostly fertilizer?

Election 2012

The Wackadoodles
(Latin: *wacus dudlei*)
are creeping out of the woodwork
and into our elections!

They are convinced
Jesus Is Coming Soon.
(If you don't believe me,
read their bumper stickers.)

If He's smart, He won't.

When He tells them to
STOP worshipping The Market,
STOP stealing
from the elderly, sick and disabled,
STOP stealing
from children, the poor & downtrodden,
STOP bullying women and gays,
STOP bullying immigrants and Muslims,
STOP bullying the working classes,

those paragons of virtue
will crucify Him all over again.

Enlightenment

Might begin with a vegetarian
of 25 years
buying a whole chicken,
boiling it and tearing the meat
off the bones into tiny pieces
for a 12-year-old fluffy black cat
named Cecilia who suffers
food allergies.

Or it might begin
with an angry anti-religionist
buying a book titled,
With Christ in the School of Prayer
for his confused and floundering
fundamentalist Christian
brother.

Epitaph

For God's sake
don't inscribe this on my tombstone,
Rest in Peace or *Be with Jesus.*

Inscribe this: *He learned to love*
in spite of Christians, Republicans
and rednecks.

Inscribe: *He knew how it felt*
to trip over his stupid heart,
to fall flat on his face,
to lie in quiet contentment all night
beside the man he loved.

Inscribe: *He learned to feel joy without shame.*

At the End of the Day

All that really matters is
the dishes are washed,
the floors are swept
and all the chores are done.

All that really matters is
that every little soul in your care
is fed, tuckered out
from the day's big fun
and sleeps peacefully
in the television's soft blue glow.

About Equality

Since mystery creates fear,
fear creates hatred,
and hatred creates violence,
let's take the mystery out of it.

Gay sex is
no more or less disgusting,
no more or less shocking,
no more or less offensive,
no more or less messy,
no more or less interesting
than what Mike Pence
or Ted Cruz
do to their wives
in the missionary position.

Ok. It may be a bit more *interesting*.

Fleas

suck.

FORE!

Some unknown neighbor
practices his swing –
golf balls litter my yard –
free cat toys

Found Poem: Homework scrap found in *Bobbs-Merrill Eighth Reader*, 1926

… life is new
… is long
… is a silly thing

… my enemy
… is in the trap
… safe for now

Full Circle

My second boyfriend turned out to be unfaithful,
controlling, verbally abusive,
threatened to burn my house down
if I went out to a club with friends.
We were together only eight months,
four of which I spent trying to convince him
we had broken up, that he should just leave
without drama or violence.

Three years after our traumatic breakup,
his mom was in the hospital, gravely ill.
He came to me in a panic, asked me to spend the night.

I agreed, but insisted we not sleep together,
leery of letting him think we might reconcile.
We talked awhile,
then I shuffled off to bed in the guest room,
dozing in and out.

In the middle of the night, the door creaked open –
he slipped into the dark room.
I pretended to be asleep, not wanting a scene.

He kissed my cheek softly,
touched my forehead, brushed my hair back,

whispered, *I love you so much,*
tucked the blanket around me,
then slipped back out.

Another year later, a new lover taught me
the flip side of controlling jealousy and obsession.
I was so upset, I couldn't stand being alone.
I drove and drove just to drive,
back and forth across the city.

I saw a light in my ex-'s window at midnight.
I knocked on his door and asked if I could spend the night.

I insisted he sleep beside me.
He held me all night long, no words or advances –

just a calm vigil – my head on his chest,
the boundaries of his arms.

How It Happens

The State declared him *disabled*,
but he is super smart and loves books and history.
He is dysfunctional in life and sorely awkward in social
 situations.
He doesn't fit anywhere
except somewhere on the Autism Spectrum.

In the harsh real world,
he isn't welcome too many places, not even family reunions –
but in the museum research library that I manage,
anyone who loves books is royalty.

He never approaches me, just goes straight to the books.
He's so near-sighted he holds the books
right up to his round granny specs to read.

His long hair is turning white.
He's big and round like Santa Claus.
He even dresses as Santa might dress at home
on the other 364 days –
perennial plaid, bright primary colors,
and the ever-present red suspenders.

He is eccentric, but so Victorian polite.
He seldom speaks, but when he does
it's with such earnestness,
such over-succinct enunciation.

His sentences are punctuated with pauses,
he pronounces each syllable
as if he invents the words as he speaks –
as if all creation hangs on a Word.

One
Morning

I was so much busier than usual in the library,
with researchers from other states,
and local folks researching genealogy.
Many scholars demanded assistance
as I rushed about in all the four directions.

He appeared in the midst of all this chaos,
and for the first time ever,
marched with purpose right up to my counter,
wearing an enigmatic, self-satisfied grin,
an omnipotent gleam in his eye.

With grand pomp and ceremony,
he held out an upturned fist,
and unfurled his fingers to reveal a perfect robin's egg.
For you, he said.

I thought, So this is how it happens.
Everyday-Santa just appears in the primordial void,
sporting John Lennon's specs and Mona Lisa's smile,
holds Brahmanda in the palm of his Orphic hand,
Pangu pops out
before you can even say *big bang*.

Leapfrog

Ratboy & I drove to Lawrence
to hear Lesléa Newman speak at KU.
Lesléa is a writer who would later appear
on the cover of *Chiron Review*.

On our way to the classroom where she was to speak,
I said to Ratboy, *I wonder if Fred Phelps will be here?*
A fat red-faced bearded man walking near us snapped,
Damn STRAIGHT he'll be here!
as he puffed up and swaggered away from us.

It should have gone without saying that
America's vile and caustic homophobic bigot –
the disbarred lawyer and Baptist preacher
who protested the funerals of gay men who died of AIDS,
who protested little Ryan White's funeral,
who faxed a drawing to President Clinton
of his mother burning in hell the day she died –
would be there with bells on to protest Lesléa's visit.

Lesléa was the most banned author of the 1990s,
author of *Heather Has Two Mommies* –
a childrens' book about a little girl
being raised by two lesbian moms.

As fans visited with Lesléa before her program,
we heard some loud, excited voices outside.
We moved to the window
to see what the commotion was on the ground
three stories below.

And there they were,
surrounded by a circle of protective policemen:
Fred Phelps' and his congregation,
faces contorted, wielding protest signs,
screaming at intellectual gay-friendly students
who were attempting to reason with them.

The protestors yelled their typical names & epithets
at gay couples who held hands, kissed,
and made out with each other
just to bait them.

Fred's wife stood on a soapbox,
her big church lady hair reaching towards Heaven.
She held a frightened shivering wiener dog,
and sang *Amazing Grace* at the top of her lungs.

Fred's teen-aged son held a crude sign,
depicting male stick figures engaging in anal sex.

Lesléa said, *Is all that for me?*
Yes, I said with a smile, *Aren't you lucky?*
  Fred Phelps came out just for you!

A bubbly effeminate gay KU student
spied Fred Jr.'s crude stick figure sign,
put his hands on his hips and said bemusedly,
Hmmm … it appears the faggots
are playing leapfrog!

Letter to Mother, 7 Years Later, Postmarked Home

Today was the seventh anniversary of your passing. It seems impossible that you've been gone that long; that it's been seven years since I've had a conversation or an argument with you, a long ride around town in the middle of the night. But what seems most impossible is that I survived and adjusted so well to your absence. I guess the human spirit is amazingly resilient, even mine. We have more power within us than we ever realize. Who knew?!? But it has been hard.

It was a terrible night that started with a phone call at one o'clock a.m. I was just leaving The Page with Lee Ann and Shon. Cousin Connie called my cell phone to say you'd gone by ambulance to the hospital. I rushed to the hospital, 45 minutes away, as fast as I could, but it was the longest drive of my life. Shon might have driven, I don't remember.

You lived 19 hours after that. Aunt Charlene stayed with you the whole time. I wasn't able to do so, and I apologize for that. I took a couple of breaks and went home to care for cats and gather my wits (which were no where to be found). Somewhere inside, I knew you were dying, but still I kept thinking you'd pull through, because you always had before.

Due to your low oxygen count, you were unable to match your thoughts to the right words. None of what you said made sense, though you were able to understand what people said to you. You were always able to say,

I love you. You said it to every member of your extended family who came to visit.

That Sunday afternoon, your sisters and brother as well as many nephews and nieces came to the hospital to say what I realize now were their good-byes. They stayed until that evening, but eventually, it was only Charlene, Connie, Sally, Shon and I in the room. About five p.m., a nurse gave you morphine. You fell in to a deep sleep. Your suffering ended then, but you hung onto life for almost six more hours. Charlene, who was a CNA, knew when the heart monitor beeped irregularly. She said softly, *It's time.* We gathered around your bed and took turns holding your hands. As life left your body, we stood there helplessly, escorted you off this planet as best we could.

Watching you die was hard enough, but even harder was gathering your belongings from the hospital room and putting them in the backseat of the car, going in to your empty house in the middle of the night. I stepped in the front door of the house I had grown up in. Sitting on the back of the sofa was our cat Buddy, a gentle blue/gray cat who was five at the time. I dropped the sack with your things. Your shoes spilled onto the floor. I stared at your shoes as the realization you would never need them again sunk in. Buddy looked at me with that beatific, loving, knowing look cats have. My knees buckled. I collapsed on the couch, threw my arms around Buddy and burst into uncontrollable sobs. I don't know if that lasted a long time or a short time, but it is the only time I remember completely losing control. Buddy didn't struggle to get away from me, and it must have been such a frightening spectacle to him. But he continued purring and let me lay there with my face buried in his soft fur as long as I needed to. You would have been proud of him.

Your death occurred in the middle of a 10-year span in which I had no spiritual belief system. I was in a nihilistic/atheistic place that was working for me at the time. It's interesting that I coped with and survived your passing without any spiritual belief system. Many people either get religion or lose it during a time like this, but your passing didn't influence my belief system either way. I coped by throwing myself into work. Keeping busy was the best therapy.

There were also a handful of friends – Aunt Charlene, Sister Sal, Lee Ann, Rusty and Dawn – who *baby-sat* me and kept tabs on me, spent time with me and made sure I didn't sink into despair. There were also Shon and Amber, who had planned to move out of my house, but postponed a move to stay nearby until they knew I'd be okay.

But not a day goes by that I don't miss you terribly. Most people find anniversaries and holidays to be difficult, but I don't. It's the everyday things ... your favorite songs on the radio, a flash of bright yellow, the phone ringing and realizing it can't be you. This doesn't just happen on Feb. 20, holidays or any special anniversary, it happens every day. Even so, it isn't a debilitating pain, just a sudden pang, a void that will always be there. Like dear Virginia said, *Sorrow is a granite slab I hug against my dead heart. The only remedy is to bear it.**

Grief becomes a part of you, something you almost cherish and nurture but don't over-indulge. It is something that becomes bearable with time. I keep my grief shut behind a door and only allow it to come out once in a while. Of course, sometimes that door flies wide open on its own.

You were my best friend. I know it isn't *cool* for a guy to admit his mother was his best friend, but you were. If there is such a thing as reincarnation, and I'm thinking maybe there is,

I feel we had many lives together. We were more than parent/child. We were soulmates. We were so different in so many ways, but the bond between us was epic. Small-minded, petty people would say I was just a *Mama's Boy*. But it was so much more than that.

I didn't get along so well with you growing up, you were Mother first, Friend, second. Our friendship happened after I grew up and learned to appreciate you for the person you were in your own right, not just as *Mike and Joe's Mom* or *Jerry's Wife*.

We became best friends, and I don't see anything wrong with that. I think it is a beatific thing when a parent and child can overcome their issues in one lifetime and become best friends. It's no easy task. No simple/small-minded people manage it. No self-centered, petty people manage it. No weak people manage it. It takes real give and take; of loving and forgiving; of downright hard work and soul-searching; of just letting go.

It would have been so much harder if I'd had terrible regrets, but I don't. We talked about our *issues* calmly. The negative issues I had with you dissipated long before you passed on. I also realized early on that you did the very best you could with what you knew and how you were taught; that you dealt with serious illness most of my growing up years and that would naturally color those years; that most issues were insignificant.

It's too easy to get bogged down in the negative, in the mistakes. I let go of them. I dwelt on the positive, happy times from my childhood through adulthood, and there were many. I dwelt on the fact that I never had to doubt for one second that my siblings and I were cherished.

I just enjoyed your company while I could. I'm so glad. It could have been so much worse.

There are, of course, things I wish I'd done differently, some things I didn't say that I assume went without saying, but wish I'd said anyway. But it's finished. I feel good about those last few years.

You loved being included in my life, being a part of my friends' lives, being accepted and adored in our little circle. No one realized how lonely and shut out you felt most of your life. You loved being part of *Chiron Review* and the poetry activities. It made you feel a part of something vital and living, that you had found your kindred spirits.

Three weeks after you passed on, I was hired to work at the museum. The job saved my sanity. It was something I could throw myself into. The cataloging, the organizing, the creating, as well as working on *Chiron* and taking care of the cats at home, kept my brain and body busy (and the bills paid) while my heart went on auto-pilot for several years.

Frazier went off the air. I remember how much you loved that show. I remembered how once, when you were sick, you taped an episode with one of *Niles'* solo bits, that you re-wound and watched that skit over and over. You hee-hawed and laughed harder and harder each time. If laughter really is the best medicine, David Hyde Pearce must have bought you at least an extra year or two!

I moved back home three years ago. It's not the same without you and Dad and the kids underfoot – too quiet – but the walls do talk. The memories and love are tangible.

Your cats are glad I'm back. They were living semi-feral outside since you left and had a couple of rough winters. Out of our 30 combined cats, Jackie Brown was the only one whose name you could recall and say in the delirium of your final hours. When you managed to say, *Jackie* ... I knew you wanted me to promise I'd take care of her and all the cats, and I did make that promise, and have kept it.

Since you left, some new cats have moved in and found sanctuary here. This is your on-going legacy – shelter for the homeless, food for the hungry, love for everyone, no one turned away, human or animal. Your attitude always made me think of some of those red letters in the Bible: What you do for the least of these, you do for Me.

Some of the older cats have passed on: Nick, Robin, Dancer, Christine, Cecilia, Jack, Ekin, Joni, Fatboy, Big Mama Naomi, Bukowski ... I miss them, but I like to think you met them at the threshold of eternity with open arms, are keeping them company now, or perhaps guided them gently to their next appointment.

Their passing was heartbreaking, but even as they left, new friends were making their way to my home. I would love for you to meet Angel, Frankie, Roxanne, Dylan Thomas, Rocky, Harley, Cornelius, Apollonia, Charlie, Oliver, Alice, Clown, Shorty, Nigella and her family.

In October 2002, someone shot Stormy in the left eye. Two days went by without anyone seeing him on the property, which was unoccupied at the time. We didn't think much about it, but on the third day, I went looking for him. I saw a black lump in a corner on the back porch. I thought he was dead. He was alive, but couldn't move. His head was bleeding. I picked up him, put him in the car and drove like a maniac to the vet, calling ahead on my cell phone.

Our vet said someone had shot Stormy in the eye with a .22. His right eye was ruined and his jaw was fractured. I didn't think he'd make it, since he was almost 10, and had lain there for at least two days, injured, without food and water. I said, *I assume all we can do is him put to sleep?* The vet said, *He could make it.* So I said, hope taking glorious flight, *Oh yes, then do what you can!* And that scrapper pulled through! It shouldn't have surprised me, remembering the life of abuse and torment he survived before you and Dad rescued him in the summer of 1993. Within a week, he was back home, eating, purring, being the big old affectionate goofball that he is. Aunt Charlene and I decided he couldn't live outside anymore, so she let him move into her guest room. She takes good care of him. Knowing how much you loved that goofy old cat, and how much he loved you, I think it makes us feel that part of you is still with us, albeit looking at us through one eye.

A week before your passing, you asked me to take care of Aunt Charlene but you acknowledged it works in reverse with her. Her commitment to caring for others is only outdone by her fierce independence.

I promised to look after Joe and Karen but was unable to save them from themselves. All I could do was back off and let them fall. Seven years later, they both seem to be finding their way back. You would be proud of them for that, but if you had survived your last illness, their shenanigans would have finished you off for sure.

I cleaned out the cellar, found the old suitcase with my sister Kristi's clothes and funeral things, that suitcase you shoved into the furthest, darkest place you could find more than 40 years ago. I dealt with it the best I could. I threw out the once-dainty clothes the mice ruined; read, for the first time in my adult life, that bundle of old cards and letters from family and friends, that outpouring of love, grief and support, not one word of which ever lifted you from that far, dark place.

I put those cards and letters, along with Kristi's baby book, her bottle, shoes and pink rattle – those painful talismans you could not bear to see even one more time – in Grandma's cedar chest. I wish there were more I could have done. But it is the most I can do, to continue holding her memory sacred, to tell you one last time her sickness and death were not your fault. Precious few babies survived spinal meningitis back then, and if any mother could have brought her through it, it would have been you.

For all the grief and sorrow you endured, something happened a year and three months after you passed that I truly believe would have wiped it all away in one cleansing fell swoop. On May 25, 2001, your first grandson, Seth, was born to Joe and his wife. Seth is handsome and bright. His eyes are alight with curiosity and an excited, ever-growing quest for knowledge and understanding. He has a zest for life that he must have inherited directly from you. And he talks too much and too loud – just like everyone in our family always has. I'd like to have a nickel for every time he is going to hear the phrase, *Let's use our "inside" voices.* How you would love this rowdy, vibrant child!

How you would love our family gatherings with the boisterous shenanigans of Seth and your other grandchildren, Kristi, Lucas and Alyssa! They are such lively little people. Sometimes when I'm watching them play, I think of how proud you would be, how joyfully you would have embraced each one of them, how eagerly they would have returned your love. Their faces are so bright, four little smiling suns rising just for us to light the terrible darkness left at your passing.

    Though your final words were gibberish, I know exactly what you were trying to say. I could see it in your frantic eyes, your last answer to that debate we'd had just a week before you left – about an afterlife. You were trying to say that this deathbed good-bye would not be final; that love never dies even if our bodies do. You wanted to reach me for just one moment in my soul's *dark night* to say that in spite of my logic and doubt, you believed in the Everlasting; that somehow in ways we cannot even fathom, we will be together again; that you needed for me to believe that, just long enough for both of us to let go. For what it's worth, I believe it now.

---

* Virginia Love Long, *Casting of the Stones,* from Squaw Winter, Kindred Spirit Press, 1987.

Letting Go

Dear Robert Cooperman,
I spilled coffee on your poems.
It wasn't just: la la la, sitting at the desk,
drinking coffee, opening mail,
& oops! spilled coffee all over the manuscripts!
No, it had to be like this:
my aunt died –
my aunt who was really my mom
since her big sister died 15 years ago to the day.
We are in the process of clearing out her house,
my brother, sister and I.
It's just across the street from my house.
On Saturday mornings, I loved to roll out of bed,
stumble over to her house with my coffee,
watch *In the Heat of the Night* with her,
play with her rambunctious kittens.
More often than not, she'd make breakfast.
She kept a big bowl of peanut M&Ms on the kitchen table for me.
I wasn't supposed to have them, but we reasoned
the protein in the peanuts balanced the sugar in the chocolate.
That bowl was never empty.
Did I already say she was more than an aunt?
That she was my neighbor and best friend
who helped generously and often with kitty & *Chiron* chores;
that every time I look across the street at her empty house
it's like a punch in the gut?

She loved pink flamingos. In my Florida travels,
I bought her kitschy pink flamingo souvenirs and post cards
for taking care of my super-sized clowder while I was gone.
She left eight cats, so now I have eight more cats –
eight promises are eight promises.
So it was a Saturday morning, eight days after her death.
I stumbled out to get the mail,
clutching my grown-up sippy-cup of coffee.
I grabbed the mail from the box, it included your poetry
    submission.
I spied the two pink flamingos that adorned my aunt's front yard,
looking so forlorn and all askew from the Kansas wind,
and decided it was time to bring them home.
I crossed the street and stupidly stuffed the cup of coffee &
mail in my big parka pocket together.
One of the flamingo's wire legs was missing.
As I remember it, I leaned to look for the all-important piece of
wire and stumbled to my knees and felt the coffee spill in my
    pocket.
An on-looker might have said, "That guy was just standing there,
staring down at some cheap-ass plastic pink flamingos
and his knees just buckled!"
That was how I spilled coffee all over a poetry submission
for the first time in 33 years, and Bob, I was so sorry,
I knelt at those flamingos and just cried.

Love Light

Their marriage was based
on mutual hatred and greed.
Neither wanted to split the assets,
so they stayed together.

Their reward was
all manner of ill health
and ulcers.

Camilla began working at love.
She read new age books
about forgiveness, letting go
and love energy.

She said, *The book said
I should visualize a pink aura
around him.
"Pink" light is "love" light.
But I just can't imagine that!
So instead, I imagine him
floating in a pool
of Pepto-Bismal.*

Medicare for All

That little phrase flies in the face
of Ayn Rand's Gospel of Selfishness,
causes the bauble-heads of conservative extremists
to spin in 360 degree circles,
squawking *Socialism!* like hysterical stuck records.

They sneer *Socialism!* like it's a bad thing,
as if it doesn't make sense,
as if isn't a rational balance,
a happy medium between the two harmful extremes
of Communism and Capitalism,

as if it isn't common sense compassion,
taking care of our families, friends and neighbors,
regardless of cost.

as if the free market isn't God,
as if there aren't more important things than money,
as if it isn't throwing the money-grubbers
out of the temple,

as if the word *business* or *profit*
should ever be associated with any vocation
holding human life, suffering and death
in the palm of its hand.

Memo to Craig, 12/1/16:
Why Line Breaks Are Life or Death

I blame Michael for making me way too aware of the significance of line breaks.

          – Craig Ashby, e-mail (the Trump Sex Doll thread), 11/30/16

According to melt-downs by some poets
                    personally experienced by Yours Truly,
    the world literally [*literarily?!*]
                        << hinges >>
                                on their beauteous
          & artful
                    poetic
              line
                            breaks.
In fact
         it was due to some primordial publisher
     long buried by the sands of time
                    chiseling some poet's raging
masterpiece into stone,
     who changed the poet's line breaks
                          that caused
the earth
        to tilt on its axis
                     and killed all
       the dinosaurs.
True story.

Messenger

The March afternoon is chilly,
but being weary of winter
I flung all the windows open anyway.

A clumsy, opalescent scarab buzzes in.
How fortunate I am to witness Lady Spring
bumble in the kitchen window.

Monster

The problem with Aileen
is that she was intensely aware
of good and evil, in herself and others.
The problem with Aileen is that she was
bursting with unbridled love and compassion.
The problem with Aileen
is that she overreached
in helping the universe balance itself out,
in regaining the power and self-esteem
that was stripped from her
so many times over.

The problem with Aileen
is that respectable men created
the monster she became –
and in their monster beat
the most human of hearts.

The problem with Aileen
is that she was not beyond redemption.

The State of Florida solved the problem of Aileen
by killing her as fast as possible,
before anyone could utter disturbing questions:

Was Aileen the victim?
Do we create our killers?

You Know You're Loved When People Are Willing to Give You the Moon

It was a late evening on North Boston Street in Stafford, Kansas, summer of 1964. I was three, Mom held me, smiling, pointing up to a full moon which seemed to be resting not that far away on the horizon. She said, *Isn't it pretty?* and I said, *Yeah, Daddy's gonna get me that to play with!*

***

In the autumn of 1995, I was dazed and befuddled at the tail-end of a wild three-year love that had picked my heart and soul clean. I gave all I had to this boy who would leave in the winter. There was no animosity, it was just done.

Our last outing was to a flea market on my late September birthday. When we were done looking, I went on to the car while he stayed behind to talk with friends.

I watched his long-legged saunter to the car. With that smile that never failed to melt me into a puddle of boneless goo, he hands me my first and only present – a globe of Earth's moon and says, *You should have **this**.*

***

It was a typical festive autumn evening, 1991, at my crowded Stone Street house. There was something going on in every corner, talking, laughing, some smoking and drinking ... but it wasn't a party, it was just that all five residents of the house had company.

Victoria Delilah and I were on the east end of the oversized living room, perched comfortably in Victorian chairs, our backs to the big picture window facing Roosevelt Junior High. We visited animatedly with Connie Star about everything under (and over) the sun, teasing her unmercifully because she was ordering everyone around, *Bring me this, get me that*.

Sylvia, the young brindle calico Connie gave me, lunged into the room carrying a steel wool scratcher in her mouth.

Connie demanded, *Somebody **get** that – she's gonna **kill** herself!*

We said, *She's okay – don't be such a mother hen!* Connie sprung all 250 pounds of her mother hen self into action, darted from the chair and chased Ms. Sylvia down, confiscating the steel wool sponge.

Victoria and I exclaimed in disbelief in our most dramatic evangelical voices: *It's a miracle! She can walk! Her legs are no longer broken! Praise be to Gawd, it's a miracle!*

Connie darted that sharp, green-eyed look, tossed her long red hair, turned her back to us, bent over and planted her thumbs in the elastic band of those plum purple stretch pants. Before we could save ourselves, down went those polyester pants and up came the fullest moon that ever rose on Great Bend, Kansas.

My Best Friend Julie Pops into a Dream in Progress a Year After Her Death

She asks for a fuzzy peach-colored coat
with fur trim she left at my house
17 years before.

I say I don't have it anymore.

She shrugs, doesn't really care.

She stands beside a tall blackboard
and hands me the white chalk.

I write, *It's been a mighty long time.*

The Non-Smoker's Right

At our parties, alcohol flowed,
music, laughter and all kinds of smoke
billowed out every window.

After she quit her own 30-year habit,
Connie complained loudly of the smoke
at these parties ...
until the time she whined,

Do you have to smoke?!?
It makes it hard to breathe!

Rusty took a puff on his cigarette,
looked her dead in the eye
and said, *Then don't.*

One of Cassandra's, er, I Mean Mother's Dire Prophecies Actually Comes True

Some day one of those hitchhikers you pick up will be a murderer!
— Elsie Jane Hathaway, summer, 1988

I first saw him in that November dream,
his gaunt skin, sickness of spirit, intense Scorpio eyes.
I felt his desire to kill, and his loneliness

Maybe I spent those summer nights
searching the city for him,
knowing he would be there on midnight streets,
walking and watching for me.

As I drove up beside him, he turned.
I asked, *Can I give you a ride?*

He said, *I don't know you,*
and got into my car.

We drove around all night.
As the story of his broken life poured out,
he never took his eyes off the road ahead.

By the light of the dashboard,
he spoke of the abuse he suffered at the hands of his father,
the abuse he witnessed his mother suffer;

of a hatred that grew stronger as he grew stronger;
of rage, murder and prison;
of madness that had haunted his 22 years;
of fights he's been in and everyone who ever hurt him.

He warned me, *You don't mess with a Scorpio.*
You can tell when I'm mad –
it's almost always when there is no moon.
You just leave when I'm mad.
I don't want to hurt you.

He didn't scare me.
He spoke of parties, pranks and mooning cops;
of sex in the back room at the country club where he works;
of girls he'd had and girls he wished he'd had;
of skinny-dipping at the sandpit.

He spoke of his girlfriend and young daughter
who might come home to him *someday;*
of his dogs and cats
with names such as King, Duke, Princess and Duchess –
his houseful of royalty.

All night he talked as I listened,
wishing I could undo the hurt he had known,
hating how life chewed him up.

The Perfect Tape

When I was in high school,
I tried to make a cassette tape
of piano music for Aunt Sue.

Our house was tiny, crowded and noisy.

I was cranky and irritable
because no one would quit talking and laughing
long enough for me to get
the perfect tape.

I eventually gave up.

Twenty-five years later, after mother's death,
I ran across the cassette in her jewelry box
while cleaning out my parents' house.

I put it in the cassette player and pushed play.

There it was, the purpose of the whole tape –
my clumsy but ambitious piano playing.
But the music was only a noisy obstacle,
as I strained my ears for the slightest hint
of Mother's voice,
her big laughter in the background;
the lively banter of my little brothers & sister;

Grandma Smith's chatter, her *Oops!* and lilting laughter
when she remembered I was recording;
the obnoxious howl of Mother's long-gone Siamese cat –
the sounds of bustling life in our home
so many years ago.

All that beautiful chattering and giggling,
was music to my ears and I realized
if it hadn't been for that damned piano music,
it would have been the perfect tape.

Proposed Legislation: Never to Forget
for Milton Meltzer (1915-2009)

I read on Facebook about some guy
who sucker punched a Nazi at a rally.
The Facebook poster, a fine poet, was distraught,
lamenting the death of free speech.
He whined, *There ought to be a law!*

I agree. In the interest of Public Health,
punching Nazis should be regulated.

It should be against the law
to face punch any Nazi
coyly hiding behind the First Amendment
more than 6,000,000 times.

6,000,001 will be considered excessive force,
punishable to the full extent of the law.

Question for the Federal Communications Commission

The waiting room was full at the veterinarian's
as I sat there with my cat Frankie,
waiting for Dr. Schrader.

Across the room was a woman
and her six-year-old son.
On her lap was a small terrier quivering with fear.

The boy began making faces and funny noises
at the dog, possibly in an attempt to calm him down
(which wasn't working).

Mom said tersely, but quietly

Stop it.

He stopped it. Then began bouncing
up and down in his chair
making some sound only little boys can make.

Mom said tersely, but quietly:
Stop it.

He starts making faces and funny noises at the dog again.
Mom says sternly, *If you don't stop it I'm
going to send you out to the car.*

This left him quiet a few seconds. Then:

Mom.

With deadly calm: What.

Is the *"a"* word a bad word?

Mom: Yes.

Boy: Is the *"b"* word a bad word?

Mom: Yes.

Boy: Is the *"c"* word a bad word?

Mom: *YES!*

Boy: Is the *"E-e-e-e-e"* word a bad word?

Mom: "Yes."

Boy: "What IS the *"e"* word?!

Road Trip: Topeka, November 29, 1997

I neglected to put film in my camera so this poem will have to do. We left for Topeka Saturday, me and my housemate Rusty and his young boyfriend. We met up with our friend Dawn, visiting her grandma in Topeka. Dawn is 22, big, beautiful, butch, blond, boisterous, happy, hyper, feisty, mischievous. On Grandma's TV a wedding photo of Dawn's aunt and her aunt's new wife, two rowdy cowgirls who found love and peace in each other's arms in Topeka, Kansas in spite of Fred Phelps. At Classics, Topeka's only gay bar, disco lights revolving, flashing, music blaring and a barful of smiling gay people, gyrating to the beat, arms flying, hips twitching. *Did you think I'd crumble / Did you think I'd lay down and die?!? Oh no not I! ... I will survive!* Dawn is delightfully tipsy. She dances and sidles suggestively up to the wallflower that is always me, leering and smiling, bumping and grinding into me. I am helpless with laughter and people are watching. There is no trace of the defeated lesbian who was ganged up on by three homophobic co-workers, accused of abusing her mentally disabled charges and fired without investigation. There is no sign of her helpless acceptance of that blatant discrimination. No evidence of the heartbreak. She twinkles and shines and sings at me, *I get knocked down / but I get up again / you're never gonna keep me down! ... I get knocked down / but I get up again / you're never gonna keep me down!* She introduces us to her best childhood friend, a cute hot young Latino boy, dressed to kill. He dances free from memories of police entrapment and harassment by Topeka cops, of the humiliation of having his name printed in the

Topeka Journal, of Fred Phelps picketing his workplace and getting him fired. There is no sign of his pain, only joyful abandon as he dances: *I get knocked down, but I get up again, you're never gonna keep me down!* I see Rusty dancing, with the courage of several Rum and Cokes. Who could guess the pain and humiliation this ever-jolly soul suffered at the hands of two violent, hate-filled gay bashers? In this place where I should be happy, hearing a song that should make me want to dance with my friends, are unannounced tears, the understanding that every gentle soul in the club is dancing as hard and as fast as they can away from relentless hatred and abuse.

Rush Hour Traffic Jam

Just past Spare's farm,
a dozen wild turkeys
loiter & meander
across Old Highway 50
as if they own it.

As far as I'm concerned,
they do.

St. John Pastoral

an April night
just cooled by short rain
almost perfect stillness,
almost perfect quiet

but cars hum down Highway 281

some lady's calling in the distance:
Here Gandolph! Here kitty kitty kitty!

someone's guffawing down the block:
it's the cowboys on the corner
laughing, talking and yelling,
Bulllllshiiittttt!

and someone's in their yard swing
softly singing an old Carter Family tune,

If He calls me I will answer,
If He calls me I will answer,
If He calls me I will answer,
I'll be somewhere workin' for my Lord.

(that's me)

What She Never Told Anyone

When I was 23, I baby-sat a doctor's children
while he and his wife went out to dinner.
Upon their return, the doctor went straight to bed.
I barely knew her, but suddenly his wife said,
I've never told anyone this.

She told me how her step-father raped her,
how the doorway of her bedroom was darkened
by the shadow of her drunken stepfather,
her little-girl life broken by the groping passion
of a respected but perverted man.

She sobbed and told me when they're 12,
little girls should sleep with dolls, dogs and cats,
not drunk daddies.

She told me how she got sick, had a stomach ache,
was pregnant at age 12.
Her mother grudgingly called a doctor.
There were complications with the birth.
Grandma said, *Let the little bastard die!*
as a 12-year-old mom lost consciousness,
to wake on a blood-soaked mattress later.

Mama and baby took a late-night ride,
as an accusing, screaming grandma
reached into the backseat to slap and hit
that 12-year-old mom,
to scream unspeakable names in her face.
The *little bastard* did die.

That little girl searched the cemetery for years
for a tiny gravestone.
Nobody told her *little bastards* didn't get gravestones.

Her mother's hate festered.
She blamed her daughter for *it,*
because when your husband is *Man of the Year,*
he is too important for a scandal,
and besides, *it* didn't really happen,
but she hated her young daughter for *it* anyway.

That episode repeated itself three years later,
except a 15-year-old mom refused to return home.

A 23-year-old woman forgave her mom and stepfather.

A 44-year-old woman tells me she loves her mother,
she tells me she still loves God.

Sometimes the Most You Can Do is Tend Your Own Little Corner of the World

You rescue whom needs rescued,
shelter whom needs sheltered,
feed whom needs fed,
love whom needs loved.

You create whatever beauty
demands to be created,
and tell whatever truth
begs to be told.

Symptomatic, or:
Is It a Coincidence this Occurred During
the George W. Bush Administration?

What does it mean when
the city/school library
discards every book
about the life and work
of Dr. Albert Schweitzer
at once?

Talking to Squirrels

The kitties went out to play
and I sat outside to enjoy
what I love most about rural Kansas –
the serenity.

It was short-lived and interrupted
by an unholy caterwauling.
Charlie, my fat fluffy orange & white cat
ran past me with a baby squirrel in his mouth.

I seldom interfere with my cats' hunting.
When I was a little boy and would get upset
when Mom's Siamese killed birds and mice,
Dad taught me, *It's Nature, you shouldn't interfere.*

I chased Charlie around the front of the house,
where the baby squirrel struggled loose & ran.
He huddled at the side of the house,
four more cats surrounded him, eyes gleaming.

Defying Dad & Nature, I scolded Charlie,
shooed the other cats away,
scooped the baby up in a bucket,
and returned him to his home
in the crook of an ancient elm.

He scampered up the tree, then right back down.
He clung to the tree upside down at my eye-level,
neck stretched, he chattered furiously,
scolded me up one side & down the other.

I said, *I know, cats are fucking assholes.*

They Don't Write Love Stories Like This Anymore
(for Ezra & Doshia)

Although no one talked about it,
my mother's parents met through a lonely hearts ad
in a western magazine.
Grandma was about 20,
lived on her father's farm in northern Louisiana.
Granddad was 34, lived in southern Kansas,
but worked on his father's flatboat
up and down rivers
between Indiana and Louisiana.

They corresponded about four years,
married in Louisiana in 1926,
settled in central Kansas.

They survived the Depression and WWII.
They also survived raising a son and seven daughters,
who blessed them with 25 grandchildren.

In 1953, Granddad retired from 20 years
of working for the Santa Fe Railroad.

When he'd come home from work,
no matter how many kids & grandkids
were bustling about the busy household,
if Grandma Herself wasn't in the living room
he'd ask, *Where is everybody?!?*

Threshold

Yellowstone is more than a federal park,
more than majestic mountains, forests, wildlife,
more than water ballets,
more than oozing, bubbling mud pots,
sulphur pools and mineral springs.

Yellowstone is Nature's laboratory,
bears witness to Earth's birth,
lays bare the heartbeat of Gaia,
living, breathing, ever-evolving Mother.

Tracy Pops into a Dream Two Years Later Just to Let Me Know

I loved him since 7th grade – it wasn't just puppy love –
at my very first sight of him my heart skipped beats,
I was struck stupid, speechless, weak in the knees –
the very best feeling life ever offers –
it continued way into my 30s.

But my life was too tame for him.
he was discontented,
always a lost boy who didn't want to find his way.
We disconnected,
he, to find excitement, always looking for a higher high,
me, for self-preservation.

The morning after that dumb out-of-blue dream,
I was devastated to find his obituary on-line:
dead at 49, two years before.

I hadn't seen him in 22 years,
but fantasized about him out there somewhere,
surely chiseled and handsome as ever at forty-something,
his face wizened just enough to make him even sexier,
his steely hazel eyes softened with the wisdom
of age & experience.

Maybe he had a wife & children,
maybe even some grandkids?

But I should have known
when he dropped by one last time in that dream,
all squeaky-clean and dressed up in a suit & tie,
it was not to tell me he'd gotten his shit together;
it was not to tell me he was on his way to a good job,
or that he was on a date
still making girls & guys weak in the knees,
still making hearts skip beats with his sly but innocent grin.

He was dressed up for church, on the way to his own funeral.

Throwing Dirt: Remembering Julie

I was only three, but I remember the day we all met. It was a spring day in 1965. Mother was hanging clothes on the line at our little house on North Boston in Stafford, Kansas. The clothesline was parallel with the alley, which ran down the block between Boston and Keystone streets. We saw a lady (Barbara) with three little girls walking up the alley. Sandy, the oldest, the laid-back mellow one, was several paces behind her mother taking time to smell the roses. Barbara was carrying Debra, who was a baby. Julie, the active one, always in a hurry and looking for trouble, was way ahead of her mom trying to hurry her up. Barbara stopped to exchange pleasantries with Mom, and three lifetime friendships were born. Barbara became my mother's best friend.

Julie's family didn't stay in town very long, but Barbara's mother lived nearby, so with that connection, we managed to keep in touch. Julie's father, Harold, worked in the oil business. He only had a third grade education, but he was one of the smartest men I ever knew. He had an in-born knowledge and wisdom as well as mathematical genius and sharp memory that brought him excellent, high-paying jobs with oil companies.

The family moved a lot, sometimes four or five times in a year. They lived all over central Kansas and Alabama. They also lived briefly in Arkansas, Louisiana, Mississippi, Texas and for the last few years, the family lived in Missouri. I was always envious of them, that they got to move around, meet different people, change scenery, see different places, live in different houses. They told me I was lucky to have roots.

They lived mostly out of state and far away, but once in the early 1970s they lived in Lyons, not too far from our hometown. One summer day Mom had a spat with Dad and decided we were going to *run away from home*. She loaded my brother and I in the car and we spent the weekend with Harold and Barbara and the girls (who were four in number by then) in Lyons. We watched wrestling with Harold, who was a giant of a man. But he was so gentle with us and had the sweetest smile and sparkling blue eyes.

One morning we sat down to breakfast with Harold and Mom said, *Good luck getting him to eat. He won't eat anything,* referring to my brother Joe. She looked into the kitchen later and was astounded to find Joe wolfing down a hearty breakfast with Harold, who was grinning from ear to ear.

My favorite memory of our family visiting their family happened somewhere down in Texas. I was about 12. They lived in a giant house that looked like a hotel, with a long, wide hall down the middle, rooms down each side, and a bathroom at the end of the hall.

One night I heard the sounds of Elvis emanating from the kitchen about three o'clock in the morning. At our house, we didn't wander about at 3 a.m., so I was intrigued and got up to see what was going on. Julie had gotten up and was fixing a fried onion and ketchup sandwich, listening to Elvis on an old record player as loud as she could get him. She made me a sandwich too, and we just sat there, eating, talking and listening to Elvis until we were ready to go back to bed. I believe it was some time during this visit that we vowed to be *friends forever*.

Though Julie's family lived in Alabama through most of our growing up years, she spent a couple of summers with her grandmother in our town. During our junior high years, we were so very rebellious together. We ran the streets of our small town late at night. We didn't get into any trouble, but it wasn't for lack of trying! There was just simply none to be had and neither one of us would have known what to do with it if we *had* found it.

I was told Julie had spinal meningitis when she was a baby and had barely survived it, that she had *brain damage*. I never saw any evidence of that. She did quit school when she was 16, but it was because big mean girls in a new school and new town were beating her up and she just thought school was *dumb*. I'm inclined to agree with her on that.

She had a profound, no-nonsense common sense, an ability to cut right through crap and always had both feet firmly on the ground. She met reality head on and didn't waste time on crazy flights of fancy. She was eager to become an adult, to be independent. She worked steadily from the time she was 16, mostly as a cook, a vocation she loved and for which she had a natural affinity. Wherever she worked, she was respected and beloved by her bosses and co-workers, once she allowed them to get to know her.

Julie started smoking when she was eight. She stole cigarettes from her parents, who forbade her to smoke. They told her, *Do as we say, not as we do!* But Julie being Julie, kept stealing cigarettes until the day her father caught her. He decided to break her of the habit right then and there. He made her smoke every single cigarette in the pack. That stubborn, mule-headed girl sat in front of him, looked him straight in the eye and smoked every single cigarette. I don't know if she got sick or not. If she did, I guarantee it wasn't in front of her dad. And it never broke her of smoking.

As long as I knew her, she carried a cigarette case and a silver Butane lighter wherever she went. The smell of Butane reminds me of the best of times and the best of friends. I don't huff Butane or anything, but when someone lights up with a Butane lighter around me, I can't help but enjoy a brief, euphoric jaunt down memory lane.

In our early 20s Julie and Debra lived for a couple of months with me in my first house when I was 22, but that didn't go so well. Some folks got the idea we should get married, and she got that idea too. I didn't agree. This, among other things, caused a rift between us. The girls moved back to Alabama and hard feelings kept us apart for awhile, but not longer than three months. Living together was a rich learning experience for all three of us.

By the next year, they were inviting me to come and stay with them, so off I went. It was during this time in Alabama that I *came out* to Julie. I wanted her to know why I didn't marry her, that I didn't want her to be hurt, and that if I wasn't gay, I'd have married her when we were 14! Maybe 12! When I finally had the nerve to say the words, she shrugged, said something like, *So? You're still my best friend.* And that was the end of it, except she was a little miffed that I didn't trust her and tell her much sooner. She felt like she should have been the *first* person I told, and she was right.

Julie and Debra lived in an apartment a mile or so out of town. They both worked in a wonderful greasy spoon called Jay's Fine Foods just down the road, in Fayette. Being a vegetarian, I lived mostly on cottage fries, which Julie and Debra brought home after work.

Julie had an old, rusty, beat-up brown clunker of a car. If I'd have called it that to her face, I'd have gotten one of her *looks*, a swift hard punch in the arm, and maybe a pretty long silent treatment. It was her very first car and she was so proud of it. She firmly believed it was the greatest automobile to ever roll off the assembly lines at Detroit.

We took that old car to the cowboy bar in Tuscaloosa on weekends. Every now and then the engine burst into flames. She'd yell, *Get out and throw dirt!* And by God, that's what we did. She'd pop the hood and all the passengers bailed out of the car, threw dirt on the engine until the fire went out, and off we'd go in the car again. I shudder to think of doing anything like that now, but every single moment during that summer in Alabama was perfect.

After six weeks, I got so homesick I went back home to Kansas and resumed my life there. But Julie and Debra weren't far behind me. Mom and I were both delighted when the entire family moved back to central Kansas in 1986. The joy was short-lived because Julie and Debra's father died suddenly of a heart attack on Dec. 21, 1986. This tragedy hit the entire family harder than a ton of bricks. Julie never got over it, and I doubt if anyone else in the family has either.

Most of the family moved on to Missouri, but Julie stayed. We enjoyed the best years of our friendship during this time, 1986-1990. We'd both grown up some, gotten over past hurts and squabbles. We went everywhere together and had so much fun. We got curly perms together (it *was* the 80s!). We attended concerts by Randy Travis, Ronnie McDowell, The Mamas and the Papas. We hung out in bars and didn't drink. We spent hours riding around, sitting in diners, coffee shops, convenience stores, just talking, sometimes not talking, just being together.

Julie loved to wait until one of our mothers approached the car to get in. She'd wait until the perfect, precise moment, and then honk the horn. She had it down to a fine art. She loved to watch them jump and exclaim, *Oh, Julie Mae!* One might think she only did this as a small child or mischievous teen-ager, but one would be wrong. She was still doing that in her 30s!

Julie and I were truly *not* drinkers, though we did drink once in a blue moon. And even though I know alcohol is bad and blah blah blah, my favorite memories of Julie are when she was drunk.

The first time Julie, Debra and I went out and Julie got drunk was in Great Bend. The party's end found us at Love's Country Store on East 10th. Deb and I went into the store for cigarettes, pop and snacks. When we came out, Julie wasn't in the car and was no where to be found! Tenth Street is the busiest street in town and bar rush had hit. As we stood there wondering how we were going to explain to Barbara that we'd lost her #2 daughter, we heard faint strains of an Olivia Newton-John song wafting from behind the store.

We ventured back there. Julie was rummaging through the store's dumpster, singing, *Let's get physical, physical, let's get physical ... physical ... let me hear your body talk, your body talk ...* We both said, *What the hell are you doing?!?* She slurred, *Mom needs boxes!* She was simply doing a good deed, gathering boxes for her mom, who was planning a move soon.

Julie was mostly a shy, reserved, no-nonsense person. She never spoke to strangers, seldom spoke unless spoken to, sometimes not even then. At the same time, she had a dry, wry, quirky, mischievous, relentless, irrepressible sense of humor, that not everyone had the pleasure of experiencing. But, when she drank, there were no *strangers,* and that aforementioned sense of humor became full-blown and *out there* for *everyone* to enjoy.

The second time we went out drinking together, which was a few years later in Pratt, Deb and I knew from experience it was necessary to baby-sit Julie and watch her every move. After a mighty battle that finally convinced her she was *not* going to drive, we ended up at Love's Country Store on South Main in the middle of the night. Debra and I walked on each side of her. The double glass doors were propped open because it was a warm night. As Debra and I entered the store on either side of her, Julie collided full-tilt into the thick metal pole separating the two doors, which none of us had seen!

As she recovered from that, stumbling into the store, mumbling about how *mean* we were, she finally stood up straight, looked up and found herself staring eyeball to eyeball with an older policeman sitting in a booth. He was smiling from ear to ear at her antics. Normally,

Julie would have been frightened speechless of that close a proximity to a policeman or *any* stranger. But on this special night, she looked him in the eye, staggered towards him, leaned on his table, totally invading his *personal space* and slurred, *They won't let me drive when they're drunk!*

In April of 1989, Julie accompanied my friend Brad and me on a road trip to Springfield, Illinois. I'd been invited to present a lecture titled *The Art of Small Press Publishing* at Sangamon State University for the *Arts in Our Own Backyard* festival. The professors/poets/editors who'd invited me to speak, Glenn Sheldon and Rane Arroyo, invited my friend Brad, Julie and I to their house for a drink when we arrived in town.

They offered us each a Screwdriver, and we drank them down. Little did Julie and I know other folks use a bit more Vodka in their Screwdrivers than we did! All seemed well until it was time to leave. I stood up, stumbled slightly forward and caught myself just before I landed head-first in Brad's lap. Julie had a similar experience in her attempt to stand up.

Julie's and my eyes locked, knowing we were both in trouble. Brad stayed behind to visit with Glenn and Rane, while Julie and I attempted to navigate our way out of the apartment with dignity and down the steep brownstone steps. We held on to each other for dear life, grasped at the hand-rail and giggled like schoolgirls as we slowly, deliberately navigated each step, one at a time. The rest of the night is a pleasant blur.

Through the 1990s, Julie and various family members moved back and forth between Kansas and Missouri, mostly settling in Springfield. In 1993, Julie married a man named Doug in Kansas. The marriage was a disaster, but after she married, predictably, our friendship changed. We stayed in contact, but went about our separate lives. Julie separated from Doug and he died shortly after, in 2001.

We had a few more good times in passing, but Julie lived and seemed far away in her latter years. She had a lot of serious health problems, including diabetes. Even so, she seemed genuinely happy during the last four years of her life with her new companion, Bobby, and their 17 dogs. Bobby treated her like a queen and made her lifelong dream of visiting Graceland come true.

During our last phone conversation a couple of months before she died, we joked with each other about how she'd become the *crazy old dog lady* and I'd become the *crazy old cat lady*. We had a good chuckle out of that, and that was the last time I talked to her.

A Toast

Pam was the little sister of my two best childhood friends,
and our mothers were best friends.
Pam and I became close too, but she was a such a wild child,
such a gypsy gadabout,
we kept in touch but seldom saw each other.

She was a unique and fascinating character
with an irresistible charisma.
One had little choice but to love her
regardless of what she said or did.
And she did say and do some shit!

Pam was a free-thinker, as independent as they come.
She followed her impulses wherever they led her –churches,
bars, jails, marriages, the Job Corp., traveling carnivals …

She landed in Kansas for a short while after her first marriage
and a devastating miscarriage.

One fall day she picked up a young hitchhiker,
they were engaged within a few days.
Then Pam became critically ill and was admitted to a hospital.
That didn't stop the wedding.

On a September afternoon in Pratt, Kansas,
a kindly old minister from a local church
married Pam, flat on her back in a hospital bed,
to a sweet, handsome, young stranger from Alabama.
I served as best man.

A nurse wheeled in a hospital snack cart
laden with sparkling grape juice, cake, mints and nuts.
Sam would not be Pam's last husband.

A couple of decades and many adventures later,
Pam died unexpectedly in her sleep at the age of 42.
Just two weeks before, she called me. I hadn't heard from her
    in years.
In the middle of that four-hour chat marathon,
she suddenly ordered me not to be sad when she passed on.

Sadness is inevitable. I'll miss her,
and be sorry to know she's not out there somewhere
stirring shit up, analyzing and cackling away at the ironies,
absurdities and hypocrisies of the human condition.

But today I smile and raise a toast to my friend Pam,
enchanted soul, liberated cosmic traveler,
as she soars, laughing, to her next appointment.

Winter Snapshot 2011

In my tiny cozy living room,
I'm surrounded by cats of many colors,
shapes and sizes –
they #OccupyTheLivingRoom in protest
of snow and winter chill.
They wash up and settle in for the night.

Roxanne, multicolored Maine Coon,
decrees Herself infinitely more important
than any MacBook,
sprawls the Entire Regal Self
across my forearms as I type.

Responsibility for all typos
may be laid at The Royal Feet.

Michael Hathaway lives in St. John, Kansas in his childhood home with his family of felines. By day, he works as Keeper of History for Stafford County, and by night edits and publishes *Chiron Review* literary journal which he founded in 1982. He's worked many day jobs to enable his poetry habit including newspaper typesetter/compositor, society editor, librarian, janitor, chauffeur, painter, wallpaperer, ladies clothing store clerk, babysitter, pet-sitter, house-sitter, and living assistant to the mentally disabled. He served 12 years on the Goodman Library city board, and currently serves as secretary/treasurer for the Stafford County Central Democratic Party. In 2008, he accidentally became an ordained minister of Spiritual Science (which has its roots in Theosophy and Gnosticism). He's had 12 books of poetry and prose published, as well as 300+ poems in journals and anthologies. He was founding chairman of Poetry Rendezvous that celebrated its 30th anniversary in 2018. For more information about *Chiron Review*: http://www.chironreview.com.

www.ingramcontent.com/pod-product-compliance
Lightning Source LLC
Chambersburg PA
CBHW020126130526
44591CB00032B/546